W9-CAE-969

The Proboscis Monkey

by Jody Sullivan Rake

Consulting Editor: Gail Saunders Smith, PhD

Consultant: Heather Leasor,
Australian National University
Canberra, Australia

Capstone
press

Mankato, Minnesota

Pebble Plus is published by Capstone Press,
151 Good Counsel Drive, P.O. Box 669, Mankato, Minnesota 56002.
www.capstonepress.com

1 2 3 4 5 6 13 12 11 10 09 08

Library of Congress Cataloging-in-Publication Data
Rake, Jody Sullivan.
    The proboscis monkey / by Jody Sullivan Rake.
    p. cm. — (Pebble Plus. Weird animals)
    Includes bibliographical references and index.
    Summary: "Simple text and photos describe the homes, bodies, behaviors, and adaptations
of Proboscis monkeys and discusses ways to protect them" — Provided by publisher.
    ISBN-13: 978-1-4296-1740-6 (hardcover)
    ISBN-10: 1-4296-1740-3 (hardcover)
    1. Proboscis monkey — Juvenile literature. I. Title. II. Series.
QL737.P93R35 2009
599.8'6 — dc22   2008003770

Editorial Credits
Jenny Marks, editor; Ted Williams and Kyle Grenz, designers; Jo Miller, photo researcher

Photo Credits
Alamy/Celia Mannings, 9; dbimages, cover; dbimages/Betty Johnson, 7
Corbis/Chris Hellier, 19; Reuters/SUPRI, 17
Getty Images Inc./National Geographic/Timothy G. Laman, 4–5, 10–11, 13, 14–15
iStockphoto/Andrew Fildes, 1
Shutterstock/clive gibson, 20–21

Note to Parents and Teachers

The Weird Animals set supports national science standards related to the characteristics
and behavior of animals. This book describes and illustrates Proboscis monkeys. The
images support early readers in understanding the text. The repetition of words and
phrases helps early readers learn new words. This book also introduces early readers
to subject-specific vocabulary words, which are defined in the Glossary section. Early
readers may need assistance to read some words and to use the Table of Contents,
Glossary, Read More, Internet Sites, and Index sections of the book.

Table of Contents

A Big-Nosed Monkey

Look at that nose!

This amazing animal

is a Proboscis monkey.

The word proboscis

means nose.

say it like this:
pruh-BOSS-kuss

Honk!

Big noses help

male Proboscis monkeys

make loud honking sounds.

Females have smaller noses.

Proboscis monkeys

are found only on Borneo.

They live in trees

near rivers and swamps.

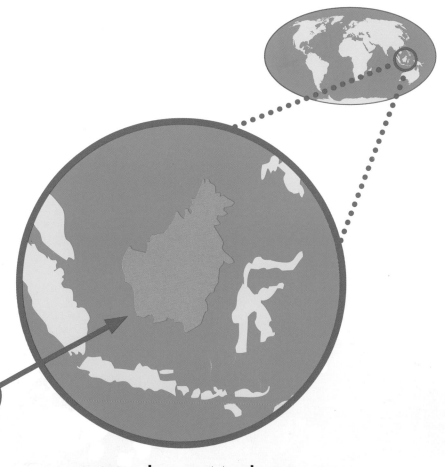

Borneo

☐ Proboscis Monkey Range

Living in the Trees

Proboscis monkeys climb and jump among the trees. They use their long tails for balance.

Proboscis monkeys leap
from trees into rivers.
Their partly webbed feet
paddle through the water.

Proboscis monkeys eat
leaves, seeds, flowers,
and unripe fruit.
Their big bellies
slowly break down food.

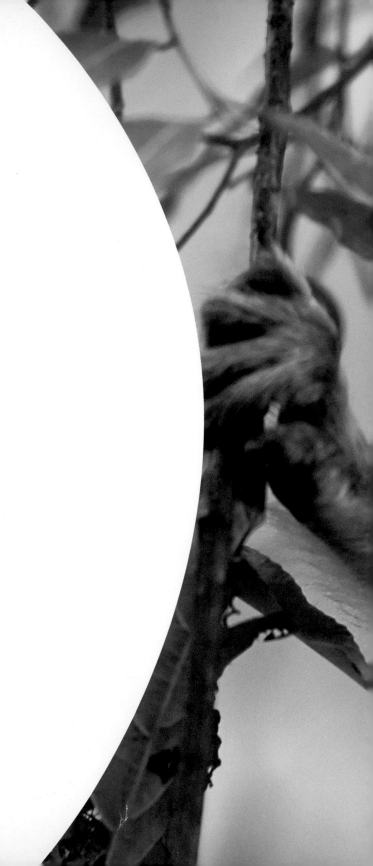

15

Life of a Proboscis Monkey

Female proboscis monkeys
give birth to one baby at a time.
Babies have dark blue faces.
Their faces turn pink
as they grow up.

Proboscis monkeys

grow up in the trees.

But their trees

are being cut down.

The monkeys are endangered.

Proboscis monkeys are weird and wonderful. Protecting their homes will help save them.

Glossary

balance — the ability to stay stable and steady

Borneo — an island in Southeast Asia; Proboscis monkeys are found only on Borneo.

endangered — at risk of dying out; Proboscis monkeys are endangered because their trees are being cut down.

leap — to jump; Proboscis monkeys can leap from treetop to treetop.

paddle — to use hands or feet to push water

proboscis — a large, flexible nose

protect — to keep safe

webbed — having skin between fingers or toes; Proboscis monkeys' webbed feet help them swim and walk over muddy ground.

Read More

Dennard, Deborah. *Monkeys*. Our Wild World. Chanhassen, Minn.: NorthWord Press, 2002.

Gerstein, Sherry. *Animal Planet: The Most Extreme Animals*. San Francisco: Jossey-Bass, 2007.

Sjonger, Rebecca. *Monkeys and Other Primates*. What Kind of Animal Is It? New York: Crabtree, 2006.

Internet Sites

FactHound offers a safe, fun way to find Internet sites related to this book. All of the sites on FactHound have been researched by our staff.

Here's how:

1. Visit *www.facthound.com*

2. Choose your grade level.

3. Type in this book ID **1429617403** for age-appropriate sites. You may also browse subjects by clicking on letters, or by clicking on pictures and words.

4. Click on the **Fetch It** button.

FactHound will fetch the best sites for you!

Index

Word Count: 147

Grade: 1

Early-Intervention Level: 20